West of House

Poems

By Patrick Kennedy

ISBN: 9780359672097

First Edition

Published by Iscariot Media, a division of Bevis Corp

This space intentionally left blank.

Cave Mouth

Shall we begin?

You stand before the entrance to a dark cave.
You can just make out the sound, somewhere within,
Of water dripping slowly into a pool.
Your torch's flame flickers in the cold wind.

Will you go in?

Double Feature

I wondered how the light
From the Biograph's marquee
Tinted the blood the night
The bystanders bent knees
To dip their handkerchiefs,
And whether he had liked
The film he'd paid his life
To see. Would he be pleased
To know it's playing now,
Downtown, in Hogan's Alley?

Ichabod's Effects

The hat which by its lack
Of head touched off the matter
Was set aside and vanished.

The witchcraft book by Mather,
The poems, the almanack,
The fire, which was famished,

Consumed. The riders' tracks
The rain abruptly banished.
And if Brom's grin or laughter

Seemed forced, well, who would ask?
He took the longer path
To church with us thereafter,

And let the old one lapse.

Night Traffic

The bats are flying backwards, all together, eyes aglow.
The fireflies that follow fleck the mirrored dark like snow.
The former with the latter and vice versa think I go;
But I am neither here nor there, and we are all alone.

The Rubble

The locals call what's left
Of what was once the world
The Rubble. Stones unfurl
For leagues both east and west
Along the ragged shore,
Where centuries of rain
And wind and waves obscure
What was from what remains.

The Temple

At last, the fog begins to thin.
The gates come into view:
Sundered a hundred years ago
By trespassers like you,
They hang ajar, their iron bars
Mangled and rusted through.

The grounds beyond are choked with weeds
From which gaunt trees strain up;
And the endless, drizzling rain has drowned
The earth in muddy cups.
No birdsong breaks the quiet here;
No beast disturbs the dusk.

Looming above this wretched garden,
Perched on a bloated mound,
The Temple like some massive vulture
Peers obscenely down.
But the wings that once spread fear are clipped
And closely folded now.

Half buried here, a broken helm
Is all your gaze unearths
To tell the tale of what befell
Both those who chose to serve
The Eye, and those who claimed they would —
Then bravely did — die first.

At your approach, the gargoyles part
Their mouths in silent screams,
And writhing forms of demons cast
In cunning bas relief
From every surface leer and lick
Their lips in lust and grief.

The doors stand open; darkness crowds
The space between. Wind moans
In broken stained glass windows where
Of old the candles shone.
The Temple beckons. Step inside
And rest your weary bones.

The Sitters

On Saturday, the Sitters,
Beneath a lowering sky,
Steal surreptitious glances,
Or else avert their eyes.

When gravity demands,
They stand, or walk to where
They have to when they have to,
Or take another chair.

They're careful not to speak
Too carefully, or think,
And sometimes chew their fingers,
And sometimes slurp their drinks.

Their ears are stuffed with beeswax,
Lest some presumptuous bird
Affront them with a song,
Or strangers want a word.

They've come to sit in these chairs;
They're so much better than
The ones at home for sitting
And doing nothing in.

The Sorcerer's Garden

The grass declines to grow or die;
Each blade is evergreen;
And every leaf of every tree,
And every flower seems
Likewise from the vagaries
Of life set free.

Fountain

A sculpted lion's face emerges from
A limestone wall; what looks like water falls
In ribbons from its darkly parted jaws,
And gurgles in a bowl between its paws.

Troll

Mottled hoary gray
And reddish brown, the skin
Looks tough but flakes away
Like bark beneath your fingers.

Hair sprouts from the head
In tangled, leaf green knots —
Except where autumn wind
Has left it bare in spots.

Tendril-like, the toes
Root among the rocks.
The light is long since gone
The arms are raised to block.

Golem

As we were walking up and down
And to and fro below the ground
(As we were wont to do), we found

A makeshift man in tattered dress.
The riddle that he posed we guessed,
Then watched as from his soulless rest

He stirred. Like lights, his eyes came on.
Our very own automaton:
He fought for us, for he was strong.

Wandering Monsters

When you are left behind
Or lost; when you can least
Afford it, some fell beast
Surprises you; the limed-

Over bones

Piece themselves back together.
You will never
Leave here alive.

Soiled

Glad of the grime today,
I do not clap it off but grind it in.
I want to press it through my pores this time,
Where maybe with what sweat I haven't shed
And all the sunbeams broken in
It will conspire to bring
Forth flowers from my head.

Flame Tongue

Sometimes it laughs a thin, shrill laugh,
Or shrieks as if in pain —
Sometimes it's hard to tell the difference;
Sometimes they sound the same.

Sometimes the wind will make it snap,
Or cause the swirling sparks
To coil and spring up suddenly
At something in the dark.

In rain or falling snow, it spits
And hisses like a snake,
But when it's calm it ripples like
The surface of a lake.

Caged behind a grate, it roars.
Asleep, it wakes if poked.
And when it dies, it dissipates
In wreaths of silent smoke.

E-3778Q-1

Mechanical parts
Click like black boots keeping time:
A clock that tells death.

Firstborn

Ruined angel, is it true
That you loved Him and He loved you
When the universe was new?

The Person from Porlock

I've heard him called a charming lie,
But the same man that Sam described
Is at my door each day —
Shouting and banging away.
"On business here!" he'll say.
And I can't concentrate.

Medusa Medici

Beneath a shadowed archway,
Her severed head in bronze
Hangs dangling by its serpent locks
From Perseus' outstretched arm.

Although her eyes are closed
In death, and he has turned
Her face away, his gaze remains
Cast safely to the ground.

Distracted by a sudden
Uneasiness, the gods
And kings arrayed before her seek
Its source unwittingly.

They do not look surprised.
Perhaps there wasn't time.
Perhaps they dashed themselves upon
The siren dark, resigned.

Her body lies forgotten
Beneath his winged heel.
Her blood gave birth to vipers in
A wasteland when it fell.

Dedication

Ye mighty bards, whose willful genius flees,
Like Icarus, the atmosphere of sense,
And hurtles headlong at the Sun, the pleas
For reason growing more and more intense
Behind you: critics everywhere agree
Your contributions constitute immense
Artisticness. And so I dedicate
This poem to you, whom readers underrate.

Resting Place

A maze of chiseled stone surrounds
This carefully plotted grove,
Where a little fountain throws
Water on which the Sun bestows
A sparkling gown.

Vanishing Point

The clouds like weary pilgrims scuff
Their feet upon the sky:
Horizon bound, where those that led
Have long ago expired.

The Horror

Just yesterday the corpse
Of Friedrich Wilhelm Murnau (whom
We thank for *Nosferatu*) was exhumed —
Decapitated, of course —
And so on and so forth.
Authorities presume
Occult involvement owing to
The presence of wax drippings at the scene.

In other news, the Wilhelm Scream
Has fallen into relative disuse
After much abuse.

The Shut-In

The former tenant, take my word,
Was good for nothing, had no friends,
No job, was neither seen nor heard
Departing or returning, tends —
Or tended, I should say — to stay
Shut up alone for years on end —
As though, we always said, he thought
Himself to good to condescend
To mingle with the common lot.

He won't be missed, I'll tell you that,
And this: whatever he was at,
Or up to, if you like, was not
For good, that much is clear. My dear,
It's getting late! Oh well, you'll fit
In nicely, I can tell. I've got
A sense for such things. Let me get
The paperwork prepared. Perhaps
You'd be so kind as to wait right here?

Necromancer

On shelves that climb the walls I keep
In covered jars the dead.
Sometimes I take one down and listen
To what, in life, it said;
Or run a reverent finger down
Its timeworn spine; or spread
Its entrails in my lap and try
To read them; but instead
Often I only want to sit
Among them, as though I
Myself were someone someone else
Would care for when I die.

Voodoo

I stab their waxwork stand-ins with
The stylus, and they scream —
In fear and pain, but also joy,
And sometimes ecstasy.

And when they're good I memorize
Each syllable by rote;
And when they're bad I sigh and slit
Their throats.

The Dreamer

A little sunlight lances through
The canopy of leaves,
Illuminating motes of dust
And glinting on his greaves.

His legs stretch out upon the ground,
His back against a tree;
His head still with his helmet on
Hangs forward, as in sleep.

A feathered shoot protrudes like some
Strange flower from his breast,
Between the fingers of a hand
Still lying where he left it.

The sword he dropped lies sheathed in rust,
His errand left undone.
His eyes are closed with lids of silk
A patient spider spun.

The Gloaming

Through cracks between the night and day,
The evening falls; the shadows prey
Like vampires in the flowerbed,
Draining the roses' precious red
Beneath their longing fangs. The Sun
Vainly resists, slowly succumbs
To subtle Gaia's need to veil
As much, in turn, as she reveals.
And by some ancient, hallowed charm,
This undecided light disarms
The senses; one can almost hear
The groaning of celestial gears.
Then as though it has all been made
Of smoke, the world evaporates.

Riddle

My paper heart has never beat.
I'm half a man, but mirrored be.
A king without a kingdom me.

Idyll

The birds' initial protests slowly fade
As I am reckoned harmless; and before
Too long the ants are eager to explore
The boundaries of my boots, so unafraid
Are they. The earth goes dark as clouds ignore
The Sun but reignites a moment later.
A scheduled rain ensues, on cue abates.

Grow Ye Dread

A car with darkened windows parked
Across the street all day.
An unsigned letter threatening
To talk unless you pay.

A sound that's probably, "You know
How these old houses are."
The man with the fedora and
That ghastly facial scar.

Two briefcases that look the same —
They must have got mixed up.
The dregs of some strange substance at
The bottom of a cup.

The chauffeur turned in early, but
His boots are scratched and muddy.
Did he use the secret passage from
The garden to the study?

The lawyer said the old man changed
His will before he died.
Was he insinuating that
It wasn't suicide?

The ocean may look lovely bathed
In moonlight, but the ground
Around the cliffs is treacherous,
And it's a long way down.

Scythe

The shimmering blades that masquerade
As men though they may not evade
Disaster's traces run in place today.

Choir

They sing at ease who dwell among the dead,
Or take the sun upon the emerald lawn,
Or nod beneath the shade-encompassed trees,
And worry not where those who went have gone.

Relic

Only the slight swell of a marble breast
Betrays her sex, for that is all that's left.
Whether the elements have taken the rest
Or vandals have defiled her, time forgets.

Alice These Days

Her face as from a pitcher poured
Forward toward her phone,
Where presently it lost within
A well of light its own.

Kaleidoscope

The flowers that depend
So lightly from the ends
Of boughs like butterflies
On tethers every time
The wind blows spring to life.

Gatecrasher

The books here have no contents;
The songs here have no say;
The flowers here refresh themselves
While I'm away.

The clocks here have no patience;
The rooms here have no roof.
I've never met the host; the guests
Are all aloof.

Pharaoh's Trunk

The day they dug the king's
Dismembered quartzite torso from the mud
And muck beneath the slum
His subjects had in his absence heaped
Like trash atop the Sun,
I couldn't help but think
They'd found the upper half of Shelley's vast
And trunkless legs at last.

Cloud Cover

After a midday spattering of rain,
The Sun peeks out, then disappears again.
Count me among the the tribe of misfits who
Prefer a world of wind and shadow to
A breathless, blinding one. Far better He
Should look away, than shine His light on me.

Windfall

The carpet of discarded yellow
Flowers gravity
And time and passing breezes heap
In piles about my feet
Are not the well-earned laurels of
A mighty victory,
But merely the reward of steady
Inactivity.

The Lemons

Abhor the vacuum; deify the dust.
Render to Caesar salad if you must.
Let bygones not be gone, and for God's sake
From whoso life should give the lemons, take them.

Creation

Behold! Where late existence advertised
A vacancy, these vulgar frames reside.
Forgive them for they know not what, nor why
They're here at all, nor anything besides.

My Cauldron

My cauldron overfloweth with
The din of many souls,
Competing with each other to
What purpose no one knows.

I spoon their boiling voices into
Ancient, leaking bowls,
And dole an empty vessel out
To every passing ghost.

The Dictator

As age eclipsed his visage, we forgot
The way the lip had curled; how at the hint
Of insolence the eyelids used to drop
Like guillotines past eyes as hard as flint.

The Veil

A single silken strand of web the wind
Is wafting up and down appears to come
And go before my eyes beneath the sun,
As if between the known world and the one
Beyond the veil were similarly thin.

Darlings

O astronauts deprived
Of oxygen; all ye escorted by
Two men in top hats to a quarry and knifed
For non-specific crimes;
Children of mine,
Condemned to wander Limbo for all time
Because unbaptized; anyone whom I
Promised some sherry then buried alive:
I'm sorry.
Though it were ill-advised,
Should lightning strike I'll try to galvanize
Your decomposing bodies back to life
Tomorrow.

Changeling

What never existed before
Thinks nothing now of opening doors,
Or hurling itself to the floor
To thrash and roar
For reasons several seconds more
Shall render unimportant.

Syzygy

Through flimsy, darkened cellophane
Arranged in squares and stuck
To no less fleeting cardboard frames,
At what one cannot look
Too long upon, we stared today.

No priests proclaimed the end was nigh;
No virgins had to die.
Our telephones had told us when
To look and where and why.
Alignments augur nothing now
We understand the sky.

Guardian Angels

Between the gentle rustling of the sea
Of emerald leaves above them and the deep,
Abiding quietude entombed beneath,
Our graven angels grieve, but cannot weep.
With folded wings, or open wide to beat
The Reaper back; with stricken gazes cast
To earth, or up to heaven to beseech
God's mercy for the children at their feet;
With empty hands outstretched, or closed upon
The hilt of Michael's sword or Gabriel's horn,
They plead for those whose cases are foregone,
And comfort those whom no one stops to mourn.

Proving Ground

The ground itself could like a mouth
Part ways beneath your feet,
And swallow you and your startled shout
In seconds flat completely.

The walls could draw like curtains closed;
The ceiling could descend
Like doom in Attic tragedy —
Inexorably: The End.

A passing gust of wind could snuff
Like candlelight your life,
Or a sip of water twist your guts
As well as any knife.

And if somehow inanimate
Antagonists had failed
To make of you a moral, then
The animate prevailed.

Dead Letters

The package I expected never came.
I posted several letters — every one
Was stamped return to sender. When I phoned
The toll-free number nobody explained.

On Hearing a Plan for the Composting of Human Remains

We ran for man as refuse out of room
So rapidly we quietly resumed
Incinerating him or her, but soon
That, too, was wisely reckoned to consume
Excessive energy; so we agreed
To make ourselves a mulch for burying seeds.

Poets

Even the good get forgotten, in time.
Only the great survive.
The bad at best are never missed;
The worst are buried alive.

Banshee

Around outside the house
She whirled and wailed and shook
The windows, wanting in.
Occasionally she hurled
Her awesome weight in one
Great gust against a door
Or wall somewhere before
Pretending to walk off.
When finally she broke
Down and began to weep,
The world went slick with grief.

Umbrella

The other day the cloud
That followed you around
Was gray; today — it's blond!
And all of your troubles are gone.

Waterfall

Flashing in the sun,
Unceasingly her tumbling
Tresses come undone.

Milord

He likes his chickens murdered,
Mashed to bits and dipped
In boiling oil, beheaded,
And smothered in ketchup.
I serve them drawn and quartered
To try and stop him gorging.
His mother thinks I worry
Too much, but I'm not sure.
Excuse me, he is screaming
In tongues to bring him more.

Taper

Shifting back and forth behind
The hollow sockets, so long blind,
The candle's flame conferred a kind
Of ersatz life upon the skull.
A rakish grin replaced the dull
But stoical expression death
Had pasted there; the pallor left
What passed for sunken cheeks; and though
The brain had burned out long ago,
The place where it had been began to glow.

Market Goblins

The goblins shave their heads to hide
Their horseshoe-pattern baldness, lave
Their sunken cheeks in cheap cologne,
Don badly tailored three-piece sheets,
And moan in corporatese.

For fun they saddle hobos, ride
Them ragged, shoot them, eat them, save
Their teeth for souvenirs; or stone
A clown to pulp for too-big feet;
Or smother chumps with fees.

Palimpsest

A densely wadded piece of paper placed
Upon the ground, subjected to a flame,
Does not flare up; instead the fire traces
A jagged line along the crumpled frame,
Then slips inside at an unhurried pace.
The paper blooms as restless atoms claim
More space, unfolding fragile petals chased
With lava forking out in tiny veins.
The dull white color drains away, replaced
By silken grey. The wind takes what remains
A cinder at a time, slowly erasing
From top to bottom till a ghostly stain
Is all that's left. At night, the rain effaces
That, too, and leaves the earth unmarked again.

Derelict

The walls or most of them
At any rate persist
In standing. Shadows list
This way or the that way when
The Sun goes up and down.
Fallen masonry drowns
In earth unhinged by rain,
And waves of grass. The black
Rectangles where great panes
Once glowed give nothing back.

Scattered Showers

The wood still drips with last
Night's rain; the same
Precipitation casts
Upon a palisade
Protecting no one now
Peculiar shade.

A willow gently waves
A knotted hand
Before a yawning cave.
You're standing in the rain.
You've washed ashore. The sand
Is black, volcanic.

The wind sends ripples through
The grass; time passes
Like rain. From this height, you
Can hear the waves complain.
The bridge that used to span
The gulf collapsed.

At night the utter dark
Like water laps
Your firelight's ragged shore.
The tortured deadwood cracks
And sends up sparks. It's fall;
The forest floor

Is thick with leaves, and sweet
With fresh decay.

Bluster

Destroy their careful hairdos, wind,
And do with as you will
Whatever stray debris defies
The autumn curfew still;
Disrobe the trees, and taunt until
Her temper flares the sea.

Sentinels

The metal men one meets upon
The battlements can neither see,
Nor smell, nor feel, nor hear, nor speak,
Nor quit their posts when we are gone,
Nor keep them willingly.

Neither the wind nor rain appears
To reck their arms, nor hesitate
The birds to make their armored pates
A moment's perch, nor children fear
To brush their hammered plate.

Epitaph

A moment of your time
Is all, dear passerby,
I ask. Alas, I've
Spent mine.

The Master

In alleys where the trash stood heaped so high
That if it fell, as he so often feared
It would, it would have buried him alive,
The Master liked to sit and stroke his beard.

Wake

The books there wasn't time
To read remained arranged,
The hands upon the antique clock unchanged.

The records in their sleeves
Slept soundly vertically
As he who loved them horizontally.

The keys he couldn't find
The doors to turned as one
To look up as the ceiling came undone.

He dwells among them now
That cannot fail to sing
The mute inscrutability of things.

The Difference

The Difference first alights
In trees whose foliage secrets it from sight,
Where suddenly the songs
Of songbirds die that lasted all day long.

Interloper

By someone yet unseen, the door —
Or by the wind, or of its own accord —
Is opened, and at once receives
As though they were expected fallen leaves.

The cold October air assumes
In seconds the dimensions of the room.
And suddenly it isn't clear
Who is and who is not intruding here.

Draft

Three pinwheels and a butterfly bereft
Of wind that weren't here before attest
To who of whom no other trace is left
(Or none that I would know from grass): a guest.

The tallest of the former turns as if
Acknowledging acknowledgement of it.
Or maybe it's responding to her breath
Whose toy it is to toy with, more or less.

Viareggio

As carefully as carelessly she'd drowned
Him one day, on another laid him down;
And as she slipped away she made the sound
A mother soothes an infant with, and frowned.

The parts left unprotected by the dress —
The face and hands, Trelawney said — were fleshless.
Still safe within the pocket near his breast
Slept Adonais, lately laid to rest.

The record doesn't specify if those
Are pearls that were his eyes or vacant holes;
Or whether the West Wind had helped to stoke
The flames or scatter sparks as he had hoped.

In Fournier's *The Funeral*, the smoke
Blends seamlessly with heaven's tattered cloak.
Good Christian men, his critics crowed and joked,
"Now he knows whether there's a God or no."

Oubliette

A well perhaps six feet across,
Unfathomably deep,
Where light that strays too far gets lost
And errant voices sleep,
And into which the wistful toss
The odd small coin, or leap,
Has for as far as anyone
Can recollect stood here,
Encircled by the whispering pines
That never venture nearer.

Elegy for a Pub

The smoke no longer spills like waterfalls
Turned upside down from nostrils rimmed with soot.
The jaws that gaped so greedily are shut.
And on the shuttered eyelids someone's scrawled
What since has ceased to appertain: "Last call."
The half-digested contents of its guts —
A magic carpet, wooden casks, and what
Was once a shining suit of armor — sprawl
Beside the brick red scales; but not one grain
Of all its golden crop of wealth remains.

Unbirthday

Inscribed upon a marble square
Beneath an unused name,
A single date commemorates
Her birth and death: the same.

The Stacks

The skeleton selected a secluded
Section of the stacks and settled down.
So awkward, he opined, to be denuded
Of flesh in public places, like some clown
In motley for the vulgar crowd's amusement.
Even the books had jackets, for Christ's sake.
The way his hips especially protruded
Embarrassed him no end. Then there was how
He *clattered* all the time. The empty space
Where once the family jewels had hung stung, too.
Thank God for "Poetry." At least he knew
No one would stumble on him here these days.

Demogorgon

Like everyone, we knew someone who knew
Someone who said they'd killed it — which if true
Meant either there were more of them than one,
Or death was something it had overcome.

Of course we never credited such clap.
We'd been as many times around the map
As anyone. We knew some people took
A shortcut, and ignored the sacred books.

That it in truth existed we inferred
From complicated signs, as priests confirm
The presence of black holes in outer space.
We never had the pleasure face to face.

As time wore on, we thought about it less
And less, and laid our innocence to rest.
Our memories grew pale and thin as spectres.
At night we woke from nightmares short of breath.

Houseguests

They wink into existence
Ex nihilo (or so
It seems to you), and if
You ask them, they won't go.

They make themselves at home,
And bogart your remote,
And leave you cryptic notes,
And commandeer your phone.

They ask you what's for breakfast,
And later on for lunch,
And tell you they had dinner
At someplace famous once.

They hope you understand:
They had no place to stay.
And anyway it's not
Like it's forever, man.

Mariner 11

According to the will of his creators
The Tin Man left the Blessed Isles at dawn.
With nothing but a pocket watch to guide him,
He waded past the breakers and was gone.
The letters in confetti he sent home
Revealed when reassembled he was lonely.
The sea it seemed stood empty, save for sparks
Too far away and few to light the darkness.
He tried as he was told to do to spend
The gold piece they had given him on friends.
Even after his battery wound down,
And he drifted with the current like a cloud,
The coin remained clasped tightly in his hand,
In hopes that someday someone would understand.

City by the Sea

The thunder of the surf
Collapsing on the shore
No longer vies with voices to
Be heard here anymore.

Disfigured by the rain
And clad in verdigris,
What people there are left maintain
Their silence rigidly.

The wind has picked the temples
And marble columns clean.
The empty portals gape like mouths
Arrested in a scream.

The vestige of a road
Heads off into the sand,
But there is nothing else besides
The sea on either hand.

Chalk Outline

The books because the shelves
Stand mostly empty now
Lay flat or falling down.
The bargain basement elves
Have picked her pinewood bones
Clean of tasty morsels,
The land sharks with their dorsal
Dollars drunk their fill.
In muted, guilty tones,
What patrons there are left
Rehash the kill.

We'll lay the dead to rest
Next week, she tells the guests
Who don't know yet, and sighs,
And lets them feign surprise.

Confession

I never meant to kill her, please
Believe me, it's the truth —
Though that she'd die if I stood by
And failed to act, I knew.

I put my hands around her neck
And twisted till it snapped,
But she was dead already when
I did it, that's a fact.

Her entrails trailing from her trunk,
I grabbed her by the hair,
And dragged her to a garbage can,
And left her lying there.

In life she'd been a prickly thing,
And never much for looks.
In death she left a hollow in
The gravel, so I took

A shovel, and I filled it in,
And said a little prayer
For absent-minded gardeners,
For all the guilt we bear.

Truffle

Excepting only twisted trees
Strategically strung out,
Whose trembling fingers test the air
In vain for leave of drought,
Nothing moves in the blackened plain
Outside the house.

But for the unforgiving Sun
By day, and in the night
The cool, chameleon moon, the sky
Stays vacant out of spite.
Either that, or the natural clouds
Have died of fright.

Inside, upon the furnishings —
Including you and I —
The cakes of dust collaborate
In whispered tones, and rise —
Unhurried by the clocks, which stopped
Abiding time.

When finally the rain arrives
In giant lemon drops,
And puddles in the pavement troughs
Of countless parking lots,
It's winter, and the water ties
The trees in knots.

The Park

The levers that control the waterfall
Won't function in high winds or after dark.
These regulations benefit us all,
And help preserve the beauty of the park.

All flowers deemed unsightly or diseased,
Or those that violate our policies,
Will be removed. For approved arrangements, see
The samples in our central office please.

The leaving here of ritual offerings,
Which may include but is not limited to
All crosses, candles, statuettes, and things
Like toys is not permitted. No balloons.

For seven days before and seven after
Acknowledged holidays, a seventh son
May without fear of censure or disaster
Adorn his family's standing stones for fun.

We have the right to uproot any tree
Whose growth encroaches on the property
Of our beloved patrons, to whom we
Remain indebted — for a modest fee.

These regulations are not all inclusive,
And may be changed at will or for a lark.
All life forms too long-lived or too obtrusive
Shall serve as a reminder to you. Hark.

After Williams

A trembling at the windowpane implied
This morning wind, and maybe rain outside.
I lay there silent, watching for some time,
Then rose and crossed the room and drew aside
The curtain, where my guess was verified.
Medieval grey filled everywhere the sky
Above, while down below the ground was dyed
Dark with the water falling from on high.
The two-year old who had materialized
Beside me bore a look of mild surprise.
"Ray," he said simply, taking in the sight.
"That's right, it's raining, buddy," I replied.
A red tricycle, glazed as advertised,
Afloat upon its tires defied the tide.

Divine Intervention

Assisted by the wind, and hence
By God Himself, my notebook attempts
Repeatedly to close. They know
What I will not admit: that though
I stared into it till the sun
Went down, there is no poem forthcoming.

Acknowledgements

The following poems first appeared in the these journals: "The Person from Porlock" in *The Road Not Taken*; "Necromancer" in *The Rotary Dial*; and "The Temple" in *The Literary Hatchet.*

The author also wishes to thank his long suffering parents, sister, wife, children, and friends.

CPSIA information can be obtained
at www.ICGtesting.com
Printed in the USA
FSHW010511051020
74464FS